Teacher Lesson Plan Book

◀ JULY 2021 – JUNE 2022 ▶

SCHOOL / COLLEGE ....

ADDRESS ....

NAME ....

2021

January

S	M	T	W	T	F	S
					1	2
3	4	5	6	7	8	9
10	11	12	13	14	15	16
17	18	19	20	21	22	23
24	25	26	27	28	29	30
31						

February

S	M	T	W	T	F	S
	1	2	3	4	5	6
7	8	9	10	11	12	13
14	15	16	17	18	19	20
21	22	23	24	25	26	27
28						

March

S	M	T	W	T	F	S
	1	2	3	4	5	6
7	8	9	10	11	12	13
14	15	16	17	18	19	20
21	22	23	24	25	26	27
28	29	30	31			

April

S	M	T	W	T	F	S
				1	2	3
4	5	6	7	8	9	10
11	12	13	14	15	16	17
18	19	20	21	22	23	24
25	26	27	28	29	30	

May

S	M	T	W	T	F	S
						1
2	3	4	5	6	7	8
9	10	11	12	13	14	15
16	17	18	19	20	21	22
23	24	25	26	27	28	29
30	31					

June

S	M	T	W	T	F	S
		1	2	3	4	5
6	7	8	9	10	11	12
13	14	15	16	17	18	19
20	21	22	23	24	25	26
27	28	29	30			

July

S	M	T	W	T	F	S
				1	2	3
4	5	6	7	8	9	10
11	12	13	14	15	16	17
18	19	20	21	22	23	24
25	26	27	28	29	30	31

August

S	M	T	W	T	F	S
1	2	3	4	5	6	7
8	9	10	11	12	13	14
15	16	17	18	19	20	21
22	23	24	25	26	27	28
29	30	31				

September

S	M	T	W	T	F	S
			1	2	3	4
5	6	7	8	9	10	11
12	13	14	15	16	17	18
19	20	21	22	23	24	25
26	27	28	29	30		

October

S	M	T	W	T	F	S
					1	2
3	4	5	6	7	8	9
10	11	12	13	14	15	16
17	18	19	20	21	22	23
24	25	26	27	28	29	30
31						

November

S	M	T	W	T	F	S
	1	2	3	4	5	6
7	8	9	10	11	12	13
14	15	16	17	18	19	20
21	22	23	24	25	26	27
28	29	30				

December

S	M	T	W	T	F	S
			1	2	3	4
5	6	7	8	9	10	11
12	13	14	15	16	17	18
19	20	21	22	23	24	25
26	27	28	29	30	31	

2021 ◀ IMPORTANT DATES ▶

January

February

March

April

May

June

July

August

September

October

November

December

2022

January

S	M	T	W	T	F	S
						1
2	3	4	5	6	7	8
9	10	11	12	13	14	15
16	17	18	19	20	21	22
23	24	25	26	27	28	29
30	31					

February

S	M	T	W	T	F	S
		1	2	3	4	5
6	7	8	9	10	11	12
13	14	15	16	17	18	19
20	21	22	23	24	25	26
27	28					

March

S	M	T	W	T	F	S
		1	2	3	4	5
6	7	8	9	10	11	12
13	14	15	16	17	18	19
20	21	22	23	24	25	26
27	28	29	30	31		

April

S	M	T	W	T	F	S
					1	2
3	4	5	6	7	8	9
10	11	12	13	14	15	16
17	18	19	20	21	22	23
24	25	26	27	28	29	30

May

S	M	T	W	T	F	S
1	2	3	4	5	6	7
8	9	10	11	12	13	14
15	16	17	18	19	20	21
22	23	24	25	26	27	28
29	30	31				

June

S	M	T	W	T	F	S
			1	2	3	4
5	6	7	8	9	10	11
12	13	14	15	16	17	18
19	20	21	22	23	24	25
26	27	28	29	30		

July

S	M	T	W	T	F	S
					1	2
3	4	5	6	7	8	9
10	11	12	13	14	15	16
17	18	19	20	21	22	23
24	25	26	27	28	29	30
31						

August

S	M	T	W	T	F	S
	1	2	3	4	5	6
7	8	9	10	11	12	13
14	15	16	17	18	19	20
21	22	23	24	25	26	27
28	29	30	31			

September

S	M27	T	W	T	F	S
				1	2	3
4	5	6	7	8	9	10
11	12	13	14	15	16	17
18	19	20	21	22	23	24
25	26	27	28	29	30	

October

S	M	T	W	T	F	S
						1
2	3	4	5	6	7	8
9	10	11	12	13	14	15
16	17	18	19	20	21	22
23	24	25	26	27	28	29
30	31					

November

S	M	T	W	T	F	S
		1	2	3	4	5
6	7	8	9	10	11	12
13	14	15	16	17	18	19
20	21	22	23	24	25	26
27	28	29	30			

December

S	M	T	W	T	F	S
				1	2	3
4	5	6	7	8	9	10
11	12	13	14	15	16	17
18	19	20	21	22	23	24
25	26	27	28	29	30	31

2022 ◀ IMPORTANT DATES ▶

January

_____
_____
_____
_____
_____
_____

February

_____
_____
_____
_____
_____
_____

March

_____
_____
_____
_____
_____
_____

April

_____
_____
_____
_____
_____
_____

May

_____
_____
_____
_____
_____
_____

June

_____
_____
_____
_____
_____
_____

July

_____
_____
_____
_____
_____
_____

August

_____
_____
_____
_____
_____
_____

September

_____
_____
_____
_____
_____
_____

October

_____
_____
_____
_____
_____
_____

November

_____
_____
_____
_____
_____
_____

December

_____
_____
_____
_____
_____
_____

Happy Birthdays

January

_____
_____
_____
_____
_____
_____

February

_____
_____
_____
_____
_____
_____

March

_____
_____
_____
_____
_____
_____

April

_____
_____
_____
_____
_____
_____

May

_____
_____
_____
_____
_____
_____

June

_____
_____
_____
_____
_____
_____

July

_____
_____
_____
_____
_____
_____

August

_____
_____
_____
_____
_____
_____

September

_____
_____
_____
_____
_____
_____

October

_____
_____
_____
_____
_____
_____

November

_____
_____
_____
_____
_____
_____

December

_____
_____
_____
_____
_____
_____

Ideas

Students'

Students' ◀ OTHER INFORMATION ▶

Student's Checklist

- ☐ **ATTENDANCE**
- ☐ **GRADE**
- ☐ **HOMEWORK**
- ☐ ....
- ☐ ....

Student													

Student's Checklist

- ☐ **ATTENDANCE**
- ☐ **GRADE**
- ☐ **HOMEWORK**
- ☐ ....
- ☐ ....

Student													

Student's Checklist

- ☐ **ATTENDANCE**
- ☐ **GRADE**
- ☐ **HOMEWORK**
- ☐ ....
- ☐ ....

Student														

Student's Checklist

- [ ] **ATTENDANCE**
- [ ] **GRADE**
- [ ] **HOMEWORK**
- [ ] ....
- [ ] ....

Student													

Student's Checklist

- ☐ **ATTENDANCE**
- ☐ **GRADE**
- ☐ **HOMEWORK**
- ☐ ....
- ☐ ....

Student														

Student's Checklist

- ☐ **ATTENDANCE**
- ☐ **GRADE**
- ☐ **HOMEWORK**
- ☐ ....
- ☐ ....

Student														

Student's Checklist

- [ ] ATTENDANCE
- [ ] GRADE
- [ ] HOMEWORK
- [ ] ....
- [ ] ....

Student												

Student's Checklist

- ☐ **ATTENDANCE**
- ☐ **GRADE**
- ☐ **HOMEWORK**
- ☐ ....
- ☐ ....

Student													

Student's Checklist

- ☐ **ATTENDANCE**
- ☐ **GRADE**
- ☐ **HOMEWORK**
- ☐ ....
- ☐ ....

Student													

Student's Checklist

- [ ] **ATTENDANCE**
- [ ] **GRADE**
- [ ] **HOMEWORK**
- [ ] ....
- [ ] ....

Student												

Student's Checklist

- ☐ **ATTENDANCE**
- ☐ **GRADE**
- ☐ **HOMEWORK**
- ☐ ....
- ☐ ....

Student												

Student's Checklist

- ☐ ATTENDANCE
- ☐ GRADE
- ☐ HOMEWORK
- ☐ ....
- ☐ ....

Student														

Student's Checklist

- ☐ **ATTENDANCE**
- ☐ **GRADE**
- ☐ **HOMEWORK**
- ☐ ....
- ☐ ....

Student														

Student's Checklist

- ☐ **ATTENDANCE**
- ☐ **GRADE**
- ☐ **HOMEWORK**
- ☐ ....
- ☐ ....

Student											

Student's Checklist

- ☐ **ATTENDANCE**
- ☐ **GRADE**
- ☐ **HOMEWORK**
- ☐ ....
- ☐ ....

Student														

Student's Checklist

- ☐ **ATTENDANCE**
- ☐ **GRADE**
- ☐ **HOMEWORK**
- ☐ ....
- ☐ ....

Student												

Student's Checklist

- ☐ **ATTENDANCE**
- ☐ **GRADE**
- ☐ **HOMEWORK**
- ☐ ....
- ☐ ....

Student													

Student's Checklist

☐ **ATTENDANCE**
☐ **GRADE**
☐ **HOMEWORK**
☐ ....
☐ ....

Student

Student's Checklist

- ☐ **ATTENDANCE**
- ☐ **GRADE**
- ☐ **HOMEWORK**
- ☐ ....
- ☐ ....

Student													

Student's Checklist

- [ ] **ATTENDANCE**
- [ ] **GRADE**
- [ ] **HOMEWORK**
- [ ] ....
- [ ] ....

Student														

Student's Checklist

- [ ] **ATTENDANCE**
- [ ] **GRADE**
- [ ] **HOMEWORK**
- [ ] ....
- [ ] ....

Student													

Student's Checklist

- ☐ **ATTENDANCE**
- ☐ **GRADE**
- ☐ **HOMEWORK**
- ☐ ....
- ☐ ....

Student											

Student's Checklist

- ☐ **ATTENDANCE**
- ☐ **GRADE**
- ☐ **HOMEWORK**
- ☐ ....
- ☐ ....

Student												

Student's Checklist

- [ ] **ATTENDANCE**
- [ ] **GRADE**
- [ ] **HOMEWORK**
- [ ] ....
- [ ] ....

Student														

Student's Checklist

- ☐ **ATTENDANCE**
- ☐ **GRADE**
- ☐ **HOMEWORK**
- ☐ ....
- ☐ ....

Student												

Student's Checklist

- ☐ **ATTENDANCE**
- ☐ **GRADE**
- ☐ **HOMEWORK**
- ☐ ....
- ☐ ....

Student													

Student's Checklist

- ☐ **ATTENDANCE**
- ☐ **GRADE**
- ☐ **HOMEWORK**
- ☐ ....
- ☐ ....

Student												

Student's Checklist

- ☐ **ATTENDANCE**
- ☐ **GRADE**
- ☐ **HOMEWORK**
- ☐ ....
- ☐ ....

Student													

Student's Checklist

- ☐ **ATTENDANCE**
- ☐ **GRADE**
- ☐ **HOMEWORK**
- ☐ ....
- ☐ ....

Student														

Student's Checklist

- ☐ **ATTENDANCE**
- ☐ **GRADE**
- ☐ **HOMEWORK**
- ☐ ....
- ☐ ....

Student											

Goal Plan

2021

July

August

September

October

November

December

2022

January

February

March

April

May

June

Brainstorming

Quarter 1

July

Goals

⇩

Objectives

August

Goals

⇩

Objectives

September

Goals

⇩

Objective

Notes

Notes

Notes

Quarter 2

October

Goals

⇓

Objectives

November

Goals

⇓

Objectives

December

Goals

⇓

Objective

Notes

Notes

Notes

Quarter 3 ◀ GOALS & OBJECTIVES ▶

Goals

⇓

Objectives

Goals

⇓

Objectives

Goals

⇓

Objective

Notes

Notes

Notes

Quarter 4

April

Goals

⇓

Objectives

May

Goals

⇓

Objectives

June

Goals

⇓

Objective

Notes

Notes

Notes

July

◄ **MONTHLY ACTION STEPS** ►

Teaching is a work of heart.

Gratitude	Challenges	Wins

ACTION STEPS	Progress	Due Date	Open
○			
○			
○			
○			
○			
○			
○			
○			
○			
○			
○			
○			
○			
○			
○			
○			
○			
○			
○			
○			
○			

Notes

July

TO-DO	Sunday	Monday	Tuesday
	4	5	6
	11	12	13
	18	19	20
	25	26	27

2021

Wednesday	Thursday	Friday	Saturday
	1	2	3
7	8	9	10
14	15	16	17
21	22	23	24
28	29	30	31

Week: ____

◄ SUBJECTS ►

	MONDAY	TUESDAY

WEDNESDAY	THURSDAY	FRIDAY

Week: ____

◀ SUBJECTS ▶

	MONDAY	TUESDAY

WEDNESDAY	THURSDAY	FRIDAY

Week: ____

◀ **SUBJECTS** ▶

	MONDAY	TUESDAY

WEDNESDAY	THURSDAY	FRIDAY

Week: _ _ _ _

◀ **SUBJECTS** ▶

	◯ MONDAY	◯ TUESDAY

WEDNESDAY	THURSDAY	FRIDAY

Week: _ _ _ _

◀ SUBJECTS ▶	⬤ MONDAY	⬤ TUESDAY

WEDNESDAY	THURSDAY	FRIDAY

August
◀ MONTHLY ACTION STEPS ▶

> 99 The influence of a good teacher can never be erased.

Gratitude	Challenges	Wins

ACTION STEPS	Progress	Due Date	Open
○			
○			
○			
○			
○			
○			
○			
○			
○			
○			
○			
○			
○			
○			
○			
○			
○			
○			
○			
○			
○			

Notes

August

TO-DO	Sunday	Monday	Tuesday
	1	2	3
	8	9	10
	15	16	17
	22	23	24
	29	30	31

2021

Wednesday	Thursday	Friday	Saturday
4	5	6	7
11	12	13	14
18	19	20	21
25	26	27	28

Week: ____

◀ **SUBJECTS** ▶	⬤ **MONDAY**	⬤ **TUESDAY**

WEDNESDAY	THURSDAY	FRIDAY

Week: _ _ _ _

◄ SUBJECTS ►

	MONDAY	TUESDAY

WEDNESDAY	THURSDAY	FRIDAY

Week: _ _ _ _

◀ SUBJECTS ▶	⬤ MONDAY	⬤ TUESDAY

WEDNESDAY	THURSDAY	FRIDAY

Week: ____

◀ SUBJECTS ▶	MONDAY	TUESDAY

WEDNESDAY	THURSDAY	FRIDAY

September

" To teach is
To touch a life forever.

Gratitude	Challenges	Wins

ACTION STEPS	Progress	Due Date	Open
○			
○			
○			
○			
○			
○			
○			
○			
○			
○			
○			
○			
○			
○			
○			
○			
○			
○			
○			
○			
○			

Notes

September

TO-DO	Sunday	Monday	Tuesday
	5	6	7
	12	13	14
	19	20	21
	26	27	28

Wednesday	Thursday	Friday	Saturday
1	2	3	4
8	9	10	11
15	16	17	18
22	23	24	25
29	30		

Week: ____

◀ **SUBJECTS** ▶

	MONDAY	TUESDAY

WEDNESDAY	THURSDAY	FRIDAY

Week: ____

◀ **SUBJECTS** ▶

	MONDAY	TUESDAY

WEDNESDAY	THURSDAY	FRIDAY

Week: _ _ _ _

◀ SUBJECTS ▶

	MONDAY	TUESDAY

WEDNESDAY	THURSDAY	FRIDAY

Week: _ _ _ _

‹ SUBJECTS ›

	MONDAY	TUESDAY

WEDNESDAY	THURSDAY	FRIDAY

Week: ____

◀ **SUBJECTS** ▶

	MONDAY	TUESDAY

WEDNESDAY	THURSDAY	FRIDAY

October

◀ MONTHLY ACTION STEPS ▶

," Go the extra mile it's never crowded.

Gratitude	Challenges	Wins

ACTION STEPS	Progress	Due Date	Open
○			
○			
○			
○			
○			
○			
○			
○			
○			
○			
○			
○			
○			
○			
○			
○			
○			
○			
○			
○			
○			

Notes

October

TO-DO	Sunday	Monday	Tuesday
	3	4	5
	10	11	12
	17	18	19
	24	25	26
	31		

2021

Wednesday	Thursday	Friday	Saturday
		1	2
6	7	8	9
13	14	15	16
20	21	22	23
27	28	29	30

Week: ____

◀ SUBJECTS ▶

	MONDAY	TUESDAY

WEDNESDAY	THURSDAY	FRIDAY

Week: _ _ _ _

◀ SUBJECTS ▶	⬤ MONDAY	⬤ TUESDAY

WEDNESDAY	THURSDAY	FRIDAY

Week: ____

◀ **SUBJECTS** ▶

	MONDAY	TUESDAY

WEDNESDAY	THURSDAY	FRIDAY

Week: _ _ _ _

◀ SUBJECTS ▶

SUBJECTS	⬤ MONDAY	⬤ TUESDAY

WEDNESDAY	THURSDAY	FRIDAY

November

◀ MONTHLY ACTION STEPS ▶

> *Our fingerprints don't fade from the lives we touch.*

Gratitude	Challenges	Wins

ACTION STEPS	Progress	Due Date	Open
○			
○			
○			
○			
○			
○			
○			
○			
○			
○			
○			
○			
○			
○			
○			
○			
○			
○			
○			
○			
○			

Notes

November

TO-DO	Sunday	Monday	Tuesday
		1	2
	7	8	9
	14	15	16
	21	22	23
	28	29	30

2021

Wednesday	Thursday	Friday	Saturday
3	4	5	6
10	11	12	13
17	18	19	20
24	25	26	27

Week: ____

‹ SUBJECTS ›

	MONDAY	TUESDAY

WEDNESDAY	THURSDAY	FRIDAY

Week: ____

◀ SUBJECTS ▶

	MONDAY	TUESDAY

WEDNESDAY	THURSDAY	FRIDAY

Week: _ _ _ _

◀ **SUBJECTS** ▶

	MONDAY	TUESDAY

WEDNESDAY	THURSDAY	FRIDAY

Week: ____

◀ **SUBJECTS** ▶

	MONDAY	TUESDAY

WEDNESDAY	THURSDAY	FRIDAY

December

◀ MONTHLY ACTION STEPS ▶

99 *Without teachers life would have no class.*

Gratitude	Challenges	Wins

ACTION STEPS	Progress	Due Date	Open
○			
○			
○			
○			
○			
○			
○			
○			
○			
○			
○			
○			
○			
○			
○			
○			
○			
○			
○			
○			

Notes

December

TO-DO	Sunday	Monday	Tuesday
	5	6	7
	12	13	14
	19	20	21
	26	27	28

2021

Wednesday	Thursday	Friday	Saturday
1	2	3	4
8	9	10	11
15	16	17	18
22	23	24	25
29	30	31	

Week: ____

◀ SUBJECTS ▶

	MONDAY	TUESDAY

WEDNESDAY	THURSDAY	FRIDAY

Week: _ _ _ _

◀ SUBJECTS ▶

	MONDAY	TUESDAY

WEDNESDAY	THURSDAY	FRIDAY

Week: _ _ _ _

◀ SUBJECTS ▶

	MONDAY	TUESDAY

WEDNESDAY	THURSDAY	FRIDAY

Week: _ _ _ _

◀ SUBJECTS ▶

	MONDAY	TUESDAY

WEDNESDAY	THURSDAY	FRIDAY

Week: ____

◀ **SUBJECTS** ▶

	MONDAY	TUESDAY

WEDNESDAY	THURSDAY	FRIDAY

January

◀ MONTHLY ACTION STEPS ▶

" *In teaching others we teach ourselves.*

Gratitude	Challenges	Wins

ACTION STEPS	Progress	Due Date	Open
○			
○			
○			
○			
○			
○			
○			
○			
○			
○			
○			
○			
○			
○			
○			
○			
○			
○			
○			
○			

Notes

January

TO-DO	Sunday	Monday	Tuesday
	2	3	4
	9	10	11
	16	17	18
	23	24	25
	30	31	

2022

Wednesday	Thursday	Friday	Saturday
			1
5	6	7	8
12	13	14	15
19	20	21	22
26	27	28	29

Week: ____

◀ SUBJECTS ▶

	MONDAY	TUESDAY

WEDNESDAY	THURSDAY	FRIDAY

Week: ____

◀ SUBJECTS ▶	MONDAY	TUESDAY

WEDNESDAY	THURSDAY	FRIDAY

Week: _ _ _ _

◀ SUBJECTS ▶

	MONDAY	TUESDAY

WEDNESDAY	THURSDAY	FRIDAY

Week: _ _ _ _

◀ SUBJECTS ▶

	◯ MONDAY	◯ TUESDAY

WEDNESDAY	THURSDAY	FRIDAY

February
◀ MONTHLY ACTION STEPS ▶

99 *It takes a big heart to help shape little minds.*

Gratitude	Challenges	Wins

ACTION STEPS	Progress	Due Date	Open
○			
○			
○			
○			
○			
○			
○			
○			
○			
○			
○			
○			
○			
○			
○			
○			
○			
○			
○			
○			

Notes

February

TO-DO	Sunday	Monday	Tuesday
			1
	6	7	8
	13	14	15
	20	21	22
	27	28	

2022

Wednesday	Thursday	Friday	Saturday
2	3	4	5
9	10	11	12
16	17	18	19
23	24	25	26

Week: _ _ _ _

◀ **SUBJECTS** ▶

	MONDAY	TUESDAY

WEDNESDAY	THURSDAY	FRIDAY

Week: _ _ _ _

◀ SUBJECTS ▶	⬤ MONDAY	⬤ TUESDAY

WEDNESDAY	THURSDAY	FRIDAY

Week: _ _ _ _

◀ SUBJECTS ▶

	MONDAY	TUESDAY

WEDNESDAY	THURSDAY	FRIDAY

Week: _ _ _ _

◀ **SUBJECTS** ▶

	MONDAY	TUESDAY

WEDNESDAY	THURSDAY	FRIDAY

March

◀ MONTHLY ACTION STEPS ▶

99 Children learn more from who you are than what you teach.

Gratitude	Challenges	Wins

ACTION STEPS	Progress	Due Date	Open
○			
○			
○			
○			
○			
○			
○			
○			
○			
○			
○			
○			
○			
○			
○			
○			
○			
○			
○			
○			
○			

Notes

March

TO-DO	Sunday	Monday	Tuesday
			1
	6	7	8
	13	14	15
	20	21	22
	27	28	29

2022

Wednesday	Thursday	Friday	Saturday
2	3	4	5
9	10	11	12
16	17	18	19
23	24	25	26
30	31		

Week: _ _ _ _

◀ SUBJECTS ▶

	MONDAY	TUESDAY

WEDNESDAY	THURSDAY	FRIDAY

Week: _____

◄ SUBJECTS ►

	⚪ MONDAY	⚪ TUESDAY

WEDNESDAY	THURSDAY	FRIDAY

Week: _ _ _ _

◀ SUBJECTS ▶

	MONDAY	TUESDAY

WEDNESDAY	THURSDAY	FRIDAY

Week: ____

◀ **SUBJECTS** ▶

	◯ MONDAY	◯ TUESDAY

WEDNESDAY	THURSDAY	FRIDAY

Week: ____

◀ SUBJECTS ▶	⬤ MONDAY	⬤ TUESDAY

WEDNESDAY	THURSDAY	FRIDAY

April

◀ **MONTHLY ACTION STEPS** ▶

99

If it doesn't challenge you it doesn't change you.

Gratitude	Challenges	Wins

ACTION STEPS	Progress	Due Date	Open
○			
○			
○			
○			
○			
○			
○			
○			
○			
○			
○			
○			
○			
○			
○			
○			
○			
○			
○			
○			

Notes

Week: ____

‹ **SUBJECTS** ›

	⬤ MONDAY	⬤ TUESDAY

WEDNESDAY	THURSDAY	FRIDAY

Week: ____

◀ SUBJECTS ▶

	MONDAY	TUESDAY

WEDNESDAY	THURSDAY	FRIDAY

Week: _ _ _ _

◀ SUBJECTS ▶

	MONDAY	TUESDAY

WEDNESDAY	THURSDAY	FRIDAY

Week: ____

◀ **SUBJECTS** ▶

	MONDAY	TUESDAY

WEDNESDAY	THURSDAY	FRIDAY

April

TO-DO	Sunday	Monday	Tuesday
	3	4	5
	10	11	12
	17	18	19
	24	25	26

2022

Wednesday	Thursday	Friday	Saturday
		1	2
6	7	8	9
13	14	15	16
20	21	22	23
27	28	29	30

May

◀ MONTHLY ACTION STEPS ▶

Gratitude	Challenges	Wins

ACTION STEPS	Progress	Due Date	Open
○			
○			
○			
○			
○			
○			
○			
○			
○			
○			
○			
○			
○			
○			
○			
○			
○			
○			
○			
○			
○			

Notes

May

TO-DO	Sunday	Monday	Tuesday
	1	2	3
	8	9	10
	15	16	17
	22	23	24
	29	30	31

2022

Wednesday	Thursday	Friday	Saturday
4	5	6	7
11	12	13	14
18	19	20	21
25	26	27	28

Week: ____

◀ SUBJECTS ▶

	MONDAY	TUESDAY

WEDNESDAY	THURSDAY	FRIDAY

Week: ____

◀ SUBJECTS ▶

	MONDAY	TUESDAY

WEDNESDAY	THURSDAY	FRIDAY

Week: ____

◄ SUBJECTS ►

	MONDAY	TUESDAY

WEDNESDAY	THURSDAY	FRIDAY

Week: ____

◀ SUBJECTS ▶

	MONDAY	TUESDAY

WEDNESDAY	THURSDAY	FRIDAY

June

◀ MONTHLY ACTION STEPS ▶

99 No one is perfect
thats why pencils have erasers.

Gratitude	Challenges	Wins

ACTION STEPS	Progress	Due Date	Open
○			
○			
○			
○			
○			
○			
○			
○			
○			
○			
○			
○			
○			
○			
○			
○			
○			
○			
○			
○			

Notes

June

TO-DO	Sunday	Monday	Tuesday
	5	6	7
	12	13	14
	19	20	21
	26	27	28

2022

Wednesday	Thursday	Friday	Saturday
1	2	3	4
8	9	10	11
15	16	17	18
22	23	24	25
29	30		

Week: ____

◄ SUBJECTS ►	⬤ MONDAY	⬤ TUESDAY

WEDNESDAY	THURSDAY	FRIDAY

Week: ____

◄ SUBJECTS ►

	MONDAY	TUESDAY

WEDNESDAY	THURSDAY	FRIDAY

Week: _ _ _ _

◀ **SUBJECTS** ▶

	MONDAY	TUESDAY

WEDNESDAY	THURSDAY	FRIDAY

Week: _ _ _ _

◀ SUBJECTS ▶	⬤ MONDAY	⬤ TUESDAY

WEDNESDAY	THURSDAY	FRIDAY

Week: _ _ _ _

◀ SUBJECTS ▶	⬤ MONDAY	⬤ TUESDAY

	WEDNESDAY		THURSDAY		

Notes

Notes

Notes

Notes

Notes

Notes

Notes

Notes

Notes

Notes

Notes

Made in the USA
Monee, IL
30 July 2021

74573877R00116